HIDING with COLORS and SHAPES

MELISSA RAÉ SHOFNER

PowerKiDS
press.

New York

Published in 2018 by The Rosen Publishing Group, Inc.
29 East 21st Street, New York, NY 10010

First Edition

Editor: Elizabeth Krajnik
Book Design: Reann Nye

Photo Credits: Cover, p. 1 Joe McDonald/Visuals Unlimited, Inc./Visuals Unlimited/Getty Images; p. 5 Dante Fenolio/Science Source/Getty Images; p. 6 brackish_nz/Shutterstock.com; p. 7 alslutsky/Shutterstock.com; p. 8 Sergey Uryadnikov/Shutterstock.com; p. 9 jgolby/Shutterstock.com; p. 10 Nick Henn/Shutterstock.com; p. 11 outdoorsman/Shutterstock.com; p. 12 Lu Yang/Shutterstock.com; p. 13 Riccardo Zambelloni/Shutterstock.com; p. 15 (red milk snake, coral snake) Matt Jeppson/Shutterstock.com; p. 15 (honeybee) Maciej Olszewski/Shutterstock.com; p. 15 (drone fly) kojihirano/Shutterstock.com; p. 15 (viceroy butterfly) Paul Reeves Photography/Shutterstock.com; p. 15 (monarch butterfly) Eleni_Mavrandoni/Shutterstock.com; pp. 16, 19 reptiles4all/Shutterstock.com; p. 17 Charles V Angelo/Science Source/Getty Images; p. 18 Rostislav Stefanek/Shutterstock.com; p. 20 (caterpillar) Christine Hoi/Shutterstock.com; p. 20 (poison dart frog) Dirk Ercken/Shutterstock.com; p. 21 JIM ZIPP/Science Source/Getty Images; p. 22 Stephen Dalton/Minden Pictures/Getty Images.

Cataloging-in-Publication Data

Names: Shofner, Melissa Raé.
Title: Hiding with colors and shapes / Melissa Raé Shofner.
Description: New York : PowerKids Press, 2018. | Series: How animals adapt to survive | Includes index.
Identifiers: ISBN 9781538328408 (pbk.) | ISBN 9781508164333 (library bound) | ISBN 9781538328460 (6 pack)
Subjects: LCSH: Camouflage (Biology)–Juvenile literature. | Protective coloration (Biology)–Juvenile literature. | Animal defenses–Juvenile literature.
Classification: LCC QL767.S56 2018 | DDC 591.47'2–dc23

Manufactured in China

ADAPT to SURVIVE

Life in the wild isn't easy. Animals must make sure their basic needs—such as food and water—are met while also dealing with their **environment**. An animal's environment may have deep water or tall trees or be very hot or very cold. It's also likely filled with hungry predators!

Luckily, animals have special **traits** called adaptations to help them survive. Adaptations are changes that happen slowly over time to make a species better suited to live in its environment. One of the coolest adaptations is called **camouflage**. This adaptation helps animals hide in their environment using colors and shapes.

Adaptation Answers

Animals adapt in many ways. In cold places, they may have layers of fat to help them stay warm. Some desert animals have extra, clear eyelids to keep sand out of their eyes.

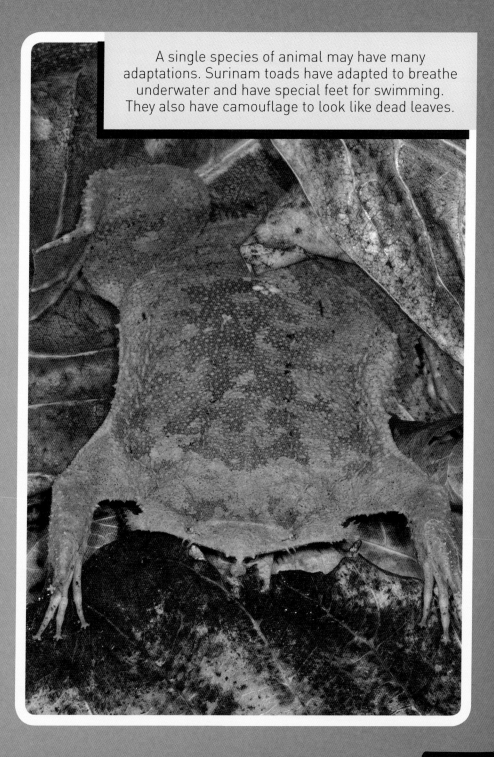

A single species of animal may have many adaptations. Surinam toads have adapted to breathe underwater and have special feet for swimming. They also have camouflage to look like dead leaves.

5

CAMOUFLAGE and NATURAL SELECTION

Camouflage increases an animal's chances of survival. It may help a **prey** animal hide from predators and stay alive. It may also help a predator find a meal by keeping it hidden from its prey.

Animals best suited to survival have a better chance of **reproducing**. Because they pass on their traits to their babies, their children will then have a better chance of surviving, reproducing, and passing on their survival traits as well.

Adaptation Answers

Some animals use shape and **texture** to conceal themselves in their **habitat**. Walkingstick bugs use this type of camouflage, which is called disguise.

Animals may be colored so they blend into their surroundings. They may also be shaped or colored to look like other animals or objects such as leaves or sticks.

VIETNAMESE MOSSY FROG

Meanwhile, animals that aren't well suited to survival have less chance of reproducing, which means their unhelpful traits are not passed on. This process is known as natural selection.

BLENDING into the BACKGROUND

One type of camouflage is called concealing coloration. This is when an animal is colored in a way that allows it to conceal, or hide, itself against the background of its habitat.

Many forest animals, such as deer and squirrels, are brown and other "earthy" colors. This helps them blend in with soil and trees. Animals that live in Arctic areas often have white fur to match their snowy environment.

Penguins' have dark feathers on their backs. This makes them harder to see to predators and prey swimming above them.

Some ocean animals, such as sharks and penguins, have a lighter-colored underside. This is called countershading. It makes it harder for predators swimming below to see them against the bright surface of the ocean.

9

ENVIRONMENTAL CHANGES

Some animals change their camouflage based on changes in their environment. This is called adaptive (or active) camouflage. Seasonal changes, such as more or less daylight and different temperatures, cause **hormone** changes in some animals. This causes their coloration to change. Adaptive camouflage usually doesn't happen overnight. Animals need to grow a new coat of fur or set of feathers.

Adaptation Answers

Chameleons don't usually change the color of their skin to camouflage themselves. Instead, they change colors to show their mood.

Arctic foxes have white fur in the fall and winter to help them hide in the snow. In the spring and summer, their brown-gray fur helps them blend in with their environment.

Some animals, such as octopuses, change their color almost instantly. This allows them to remain camouflaged as they move around their environment. Others, such as chameleons, change color quickly by using special muscles to move different amounts of pigmented, or colored, cells beneath their skin.

STANDING OUT, BLENDING IN

Zebras are well known for their black-and-white striped coats. This bold color combination certainly makes them stand out. Zebra stripes are actually a type of camouflage called disruptive coloration.

Adaptation Answers

Like human fingerprints, each zebra's stripes are one of a kind. No two zebras have the same pattern of stripes.

Leopards also use disruptive coloration. Their spots make it hard for prey to see their shape, especially when the cats are hiding in shady spots.

When many zebras stand together in a herd, the shapes of their bodies blend together. This adaptation makes it hard for hungry predators, such as leopards, to tell where one zebra ends and another begins. It's not easy for a predator to attack its prey when it can't figure out where the weakest zebra is within a herd.

Zebra stripes may also make them look less tasty to smaller predators, such as bloodsucking horseflies.

13

LOOK-ALIKES

Mimicry is a type of camouflage in which members of one species have adapted to mimic, or look and act like, members of another species. Some species have adapted to mimic objects in their habitat.

In Batesian mimicry, a harmless species adapts to look like a dangerous, or harmful, species. Animals learn to stay away from dangerous species. For instance, predators stay away from harmless milk snakes because they mimic the colors of deadly coral snakes. There are actually several species of snakes that mimic the coral snake. The model and mimic aren't **identical**, but most predators would rather be safe than sorry.

Adaptation Answers

Batesian mimicry is named after H. W. Bates, the English scientist who discovered it.

mimic
DRONE FLY

HONEYBEE
model

mimic
VICEROY BUTTERFLY

MONARCH BUTTERFLY
model

mimic
RED MILK SNAKE

CORAL SNAKE
model

MIMICRY for HIDING and HUNTING

Leaf-tailed geckos use a **protective** form of mimicry. As the gecko's name suggests, the tail of this lizard looks just like a leaf! By mimicking an object in its environment, the leaf-tailed gecko is able to hide from predators. To conceal themselves more, they flatten their body against a tree to hide their shadow and make blending complete.

Adaptation Answers

If a predator catches a leaf-tailed gecko by the tail, the gecko's tail may drop off so it can escape. Don't worry—it doesn't hurt, and the tail grows back.

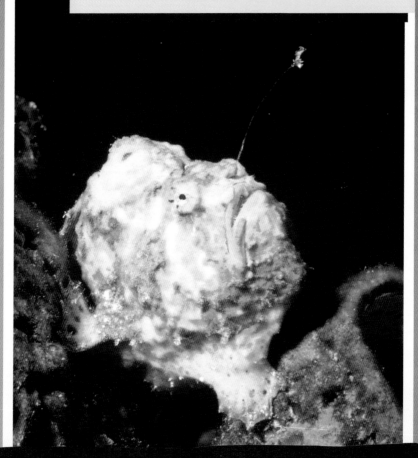

Small fish are drawn in by a wormlike body part hanging from the longlure frogfish's head. When they move in to eat the "worm," they are swallowed by the frogfish instead.

Some predators use camouflage called **aggressive** mimicry. In this adaptation, a predator mimics either the species it preys upon or a species that does not frighten its prey. By looking harmless, these camouflaged predators are able to creep up and surprise their prey.

HEY! OVER HERE!

An animal's coloring isn't always used to help it hide. Sometimes a species will adapt using colors that stand out. Blue-tailed skinks, for example, have a long blue tail that's easy to see against the plants and trees of their habitat. This is called **alluring** coloration.

Graylings are dull-colored fish with brightly colored fins. This alluring coloration directs a predator's attention to their fins instead of their body. A harmless fin attack gives a grayling time to swim away.

Having a brightly colored tail may not seem like a good survival plan, but alluring coloration fools other animals. It directs a predator's attention away from other parts of an animal where important body parts, such as the heart, are located. Blue-tailed skinks can drop their tail and get away if a predator attacks.

BLUE-TAILED SKINK

ELEPHANT HAWK MOTH CATERPILLAR

Some bird species have special coloration that can only be seen when they're in motion. Often, this means they have lighter feathers hidden beneath darker feathers. These birds direct a predator's attention away from their nest of eggs or babies by taking flight and flashing their lighter-colored feathers.

POISON DART FROG

Adaptation Answers

Some animals use color as a warning. Poison dart frogs' bright skin warns predators that they're poisonous. Others adapt to look scarier. Some caterpillars, such as the elephant hawk moth caterpillar, have markings that make them look like a snake!

The eastern towhee has white tail feathers that flash to distract predators, such as hawks, as they fly.

After leading a predator far enough away, the bird rests in a tree, tucks away its feathers, and hides until the danger passes. Some species of fish also use this method, showing or hiding their flashy or brightly colored fins as needed.

THE CASE of the PEPPERED MOTH

At one time, most peppered moths in England were a light gray color with black markings. This allowed the moths to be camouflaged against tree trunks in their habitat. Very few of the moths were completely dark.

In the 1800s, during the Industrial Revolution, dark smoke and ash from factories covered the bark of trees. The lighter moths were unable to hide against the darker bark and were eaten by predators in greater numbers. The naturally dark moths survived. They passed on their traits to their young.

Years later, when soot lessened and the tree bark turned lighter again, the lighter peppered moths made a comeback.

aggressive: Showing a readiness to attack.

alluring: Strongly attractive.

camouflage: Colors or shapes on animals that allow them to blend in with their surroundings, or to use these colors or shapes to blend in.

environment: The conditions that surround a living thing and affect the way it lives.

habitat: The natural home for plants, animals, and other living things.

hormone: A chemical in your body that controls the activities of certain organs and tissues.

identical: Exactly the same.

prey: An animal hunted by other animals for food or to hunt or kill something for food.

protective: Showing a strong wish to keep someone or something safe from harm.

reproduce: To have babies.

species: A group of plants or animals that are all the same kind.

texture: How something feels when you touch it.

trait: A quality that makes one person or thing different from another.

Due to the changing nature of Internet links, PowerKids Press has developed an online list of websites related to the subject of this book. This site is updated regularly. Please use this link to access the list: www.powerkidslinks.com/haas/color